THE
CARRUTHERS FAMILY.

AN INTERESTING RECORD.

BY THE VERY REV. JOHN GILLESPIE,
LL D

THE CARRUTHERS FAMILY.

AN INTERESTING RECORD

By THE VERY REV. JOHN GILLESPIE
LL.D

The founder of this family was one Ruther, who is believed to have come to this country at the time of the Norman conquest, and to have settled at a place called Carruthers in the parish of Middlebie. He built a fort there on the height above the site of the ancient hamlet of Carruthers, and to this fort was given the name of Caer-ruthers (from the Saxon name Caer, a fort) that is the fort or stronghold of Ruther. At the time surnames were adopted this came to be that of the family, and it is found under a variety of forms, such as Carruvers, Carrudders, Caerruthers, Carruthers, etc. Carruthers was a separate parish until 1609 when it with Middlebie and Pennersax, were united into one parish. The property of Carruthers seems to have remained in the possession of the family for a comparatively short period for we find it ere long owned by the Earl of Bothwell

However so early as 1306, Robert Bruce gave a charter to Thomas, son of John de Carruthers of the lands of Musfolds (Morswald) called Fretways. The same king gave the same Thomas a further grant of lands in the valley of the Annan which belonged to Robert de Applingden in right of his wife Johanna, daughter of the said Robert de Applingden, on payment at Lochmaben of one penny at the festival of John the Baptist. This was no doubt some place celebrated for its apple trees, probably about Applegarth, which means an enclosure of apple trees. Thus the family settled at

Mouswald at the beginning of the fourteenth century, and shortly thereafter built the old tower at Mouswald Place, the remains of which are still standing. This continued to be the residence and headquarters of the chiefs of the family for nearly three centuries. The property was apparently not an extensive one at first, but it was frequently added to by grants from successive sovereigns until the possessions of the family were not only numerous and extensive, but were also situated in all parts of Annandale. About a quarter of a century after the family settled at Mouswald the Holmains branch of the family was founded, the history of which we shall trace by-and-by.

The first accession was made in 1349, when David II., as Lord of Annandale, gave a charter to William de Carruthers of the lands of Middleby and patronage of said church, then in the hands of the Crown by the forfeiture of Thomas de Lindesay, who had taken part with the English against his natural sovereign David II. Another large addition was made in 1411, when Archibald Earl of Douglas, Lord of Galloway and Annandale, gave to Simon de Carruthers of Mouswald, his shield bearer, a grant of the following lands:—Lands of Mouswald Middleby and Dornock, with the patronage of the said parish churches, the lands of Hetland Hill, Logan tenement, Hodholm (Hoddom), Tunvigath (Tundergarth), Westwood, and Rocklif, all holden of the granter and rendering as follows, viz., Mouswald Hetland Hill and Logan tenement, three silver pennies yearly, and for the rest the services use and wont. The place called Logan tenement in this charter was in the neighbourhood of Moffat, and comprised the farms of Craigbeck, Breconside, Logan, Woodhead, Logan Woodfoot, and Crofthead. The estate was called the Procornal or Logan, and on it are still to be seen the remains of a small keep called the Cornal Tower.

From a deed dated 31st August 1489 we learn that John de Carruthers, laird of Mouswald, had lent John Halliday of Hodholm the sum of £10 when the latter was in

difficulties or, as it is expressed in the document, in his "grete my-er," and in consequence thereof John Halliday wadsets (a Scotch law term for a mortgage or pledge of real property) to Carruthers his lands called Holcroft, a coteland which was sometime William of Johnstone's, and two oxgang of land which is called the Tynkler's lands in the tenement of Hodholm. In 1449 Elizabeth Dinwoodie, widow of Andrew de Carruthers gave a grant to John de Carruthers of the lands of Hout Quhat (How-what), Stanneras, and Wamfra, and this grant was confirmed by the King's license and consequent charter. Thus at this early date the family got possessions in the parish of Wamphray where there is still a branch of the family.

The next step which falls to be noticed was an important one for the family, and shows the important position which it had attained. We have seen that one property after another had been acquired until they had possessions in Annandale from Moffat in the north to Dornock in the south. In 1452 these were consolidated by the erection of them into a barony called the Barony of Carruthers or the barony of Mouswald. The charter constituting them into a barony was granted by James II. to John de Carruthers, and the only lands mentioned in it which are not specified in previous deeds are those of Cummertrees. It does not lie within the scope of the present paper to particularise the advantages which flowed from the erection of a property into a barony, but we may remark that they were very considerable.

John de Carruthers seems to have been succeeded by his son Sir Simon Carruthers who married a daughter of Douglas of Drumlanrig. He was Warden Defender of the western marches, and was killed at the battle of Kirtle in 1484. This is believed to have been the Sir Simon whose statue composed of red freestone is in the churchyard of Mouswald—his head pillowed, his feet on a lion, and his hands in the posture of supplication. There was also at one time in the same churchyard a statue of his wife but the material of which it was formed being freestone or other stone of a light colour,

the villagers were animated by such a
utilitarian spirit that they gradually broke
it up and used it for ornamenting their
hearth-stones and door-steps

The next incident which calls for notice
in the history of the family is rather of an
amusing character and will help to relieve
the foregoing dry details. It was a sort of
breach of promise of marriage case! We are
apt to regard such processes as purely
modern institutions but they are not so,
for there was a breach of promise case in
the Carruthers family so long since as 400
years ago. The circumstances were these—
Simon de Carruthers, eldest son of Archibald
de Carruthers of Mouswald, or—as he would
be styled according to modern phraseology—
Simon Carruthers, younger of Mouswald,
was engaged to be married to Eufame
(Eufania) daughter of John Lord
Carlyle, who resided in the castle of Torthor-
wald and was the owner of the surrounding
property. We do not know whether it was
the custom in those times for young ladies'
fathers to pay over to their prospective sons-
in-law a portion of their daughters' dowry
before the marriage took place but at all
events this was done in this particular in-
stance for Lord Carlyle paid to the father of
the bridegroom 400 merks Scots which is
equivalent to £22 3s sterling. But the father
having died the marriage for some unex-
plained reason did not take place and Lord
Carlyle raised an action against Mr Simon
for repetition or repayment of the £22 3s.
This may appear at the present day a small
sum to make a fuss about, and indeed it
may seem a small dowry for a Lord to give
with his daughter. But that relatively to
the value of money in those days Miss Carlyle was not 'a penniless lass with a lang
pedigree' may be inferred from the fact that
upwards of a century and a quarter after this
happened—viz in 1617—the annual value of
the whole of Annandale was less than four
times that amount or exactly £85 10s. Lord
Carlyle sought only the repayment of his
money and did not sue the faithless young
laird for any sum as solatium for his
daughter's wounded feelings. Indeed, from

the fact that the pecuniary transaction was
between the parents, and from what we know
of the fashion of the times in these matters
it is probable the projected marriage was a
purely family arrangement and that there
was no feeling in the matter The case was
three times before the Court, and at length,
after the proverbial ' law s delay," decreet
was given against the defender for the
money.

An addition was made to the Mouswald
property in 1499 in the grant by Adam de
Kyrkepatrick of Pennersax (Pennersaughs in
Middlebie) with a precept of James IV for
passing a charter in favour of Simon de Carruthers of Mouswald and his heirs for the
lands of Pennersax and patronage of the
church. It was probably this grant which
led to the murder of the Laird of Mouswald
in 1504 The accused parties were Stephen
Johnstone and Thomas Bell or Currie (probably one of the Bells of Middlebie clan). The
Laird of Castlemilk became surety in £100
Scots—this is £8 6s 8d sterling—for the appearance of Bell But when the day of trial
came round neither of the accused parties
appeared, consequently they were de-
nounced at the bar as rebels, and the Laird
of Castlemilk had to pay the amount lodged
in security

The last male member of the Mouswald
family of Carruthers was Simon Carruthers
who died in 1548 He is believed to have
been killed in a Border raid by the " Thieves
of the Marche." He left two daughters but
no son, and on the 13th August 1548 at the
Abbey of Haddingtown, Queen Mary granted
by letter of gift ward and marriage of his
two daughters to Sir James Douglas of
Drumlanrig Questions arose whether the
two daughters Janet and Marion became
co-heiresses of the barony, or whether it
passed under an entail executed in 1544 to
the heir male, who is said at this time to
have been John Carruthers of Woodfoot,
near Moffat A lawsuit ensued, in which Sir
James Douglas was ultimately successful by
bargaining for a small sum with the heir
male, who probably could not carry on the
contest as appears from a subsequent deed
The entail was set aside and the young

ladies became co-heiresses, though as events turned out, it would probably have been better for them had they lost the suit. Their guardian married in 1560 Janet the elder of the sisters to Thomas Rourson of Bardannoch, a neighbour laird, and at the time Douglas got the lady to make over to himself the half of Mouswald and the estates of Simon, her father. The reasons given in the deed for the lady relinquishing her property rather suggest a grasping intention on the part of the guardian, as they seem to have been inserted to give a plausible appearance to the transaction. The principal reasons assigned why she took the step are —(1) That the property was in such a troublous country that her father got little profit out of it, (2) that he had been the means of defeating the heir male in the lawsuit (3) that he had brought up her and her sister, having provided them with meat drink and clothing and other necessars her be the space of zeires bipast " and (4) he had found her a husband in the person of Thomas Roreson, and had undertaken to secure for them the five pound land of Dinnragane, with the pertinents lying in the parish of Glencairn besides, to pay with the said Janet in name of tocher to the said Roreson the sum of one thousand marks. In addition he became bound to keep her, her husband and servants for the space of two years after their marriage. Thomas Roreson the gentleman selected as Janet Carruthers' husband, was forfeited for coming at Edinburgh in 1581 that is, 21 years after the marriage. Sir James Douglas got a confirmation from the Queen of the deed

Her guardian kept the other sister in close custody. He offered her as a husband John M'Math, son and heir of Jamie M'Math of Dalpedder. She being possessed of more resolution and spirit than her sister Janet, refused to be married to the person offered to her as a husband. Douglas got her bound over in 1563 that she would not marry ' ane traitor or outher broken man of the country " She was much betriended by her uncle Charles Murray of Cokpule, who resided at Comlongan. Harassed on every side by Sir James Douglas she is said to have committed suicide by throwing herself over

the walls of the Castle of Comlongan. There
was a tradition that there was an element of
foul play in the case. Sir James Douglas
became possessed of the second half of the
barony of Mouswald, or of Carruthers, as it
was variously termed, which explains the
Drumlanrig branch of the Douglases owning
subsequently so much property in that part
of the county

We will return to the Holmendis family,
who, in 1425, had got a confirmation of their
charters. John de Carruthers got a Brief
of Perambulation of the Lands of Blackwood
in Ruthwell in 1476. Corrie or Corrie having joined the rebellious Earl of Douglas,
who was defeated at Lochmaben in 1484, his
estates were granted to Holmends. Probably there was some limitation to the grant,
as these lands were shortly afterwards re-
stored to the family of Corrie, and, along with
Newbie, carried into the family of Johnstone
of Annandale by a marriage with the
heiress of the Corries. His son John married Blanche, daughter of Sir John Murray
of Cockpule about 1504. Their eldest son
got a renewal of his charters under the
Great Seal on 21st May 1523, but he died
early, and was succeeded by his brother
George. In addition to the lands formerly
mentioned in their charters those of Altowne
and Errschebank or Archbank, near Moffat
and Copewood in Dryfesdale, are included
in these charters of 1523. The Moffat lands
were, however, sold or otherwise alienated
about 1546. In 1547, Holmends submitted
to the army of Henry VIII which overran
Annandale under Lord Wharton, and became bound to the English king's service
with 162 men on his estates. There was a
third son William from whom the family
of Carruthers of Dormont is believed to be
descended. We do not know who George's
wife was, but in 1573, his son John married
Nicholas, sister to Sir Alexander Jardine of
Applegirth

In 1585 John Carruthers of Holmends was
captain of a troop of cavalry, and his son
Charles a cornet in Lord Maxwell's army,
which went to Stirling. About 1597 John
Carruthers granted Creive and Crossdykes

to Armstrong son or nephew of the celebrated Kinmont Willie

John Carruthers was succeeded by his
son John, who married in 1604, Agnes,
daughter of George Douglas of Parkhead
Then second son James married Margaret,
daughter of Sir James Lockhart of Lee, in
1635 and from the second son of this James
the family of Carruthers of Denbie is descended The eldest son of John and Miss
Douglas married Helen daughter of Sir
John Grierson of Lag and secondly, Margaret, daughter of Callender of Craigtown.
His son George married a cousin from
Denby and then eldest son married Rachael
daughter of James Douglas of Dornock The
son of John and Miss Douglas also John,
the last Carruthers of Holmends succeeded
in 1734, and married Charlotte daughter of
Sir Robert Laurie of Maxwelton They had
seven daughters, but no son and Holmends
sold the estate to Mr Macrae

THE DORMONT FAMILY

William the third son of John who succeeded to Holmends in 1523 got a charter
from his father of the lands of Corshopeland
His son Christopher got the lands of Hardgrave from Sir James Johnstone of Dun-
kelhe in 1592 He had previously in 1585
in the Holmends troop of cavalry accom-
panied Lord Maxwell to Stirling and is
mentioned in the Act of Parliament
enumerating the gentlemen pardoned
However, after the gift of Hardgrave he
seemed to have become a partizan of the
Johnstone family and assisted them against
Lord Maxwell at the battle of Dryfe Sands
in 1593 He also helped the Johnstones in
the burning of Lochmaben kirk, and his
name appears on the list of those pardoned
His son Francis was returned heir to his
father in 1619 Francis son John married
Katherine Harris, and from their third son
Robert the late Dr Carruthers of Inverness
is said to be descended Francis' eldest
son John married twice and his only son
married Miss Bell, heiress of Winterhopehead. John Carruthers died in 1722, and

was succeeded in Dormont and Winterhopehead by his son Francis, who married, in 1731, Margaret, daughter of Sir Alexander Maxwell of Monreith, but they had no family, and he left the estates to his brother William, who married Henrietta, daughter of William Aikman, Esquire of Carney. Then eldest son, William Aikman Carruthers, Esquire, was twice married. There was no issue from the first marriage, and he married secondly Mary Anne Arthington, heiress of Arthington Hall, Yorkshire. He was succeeded by the late William Thomas Carruthers, Esquire of Dormont and Arthington, who married Susan, daughter of Maclachlan of Maclachlan, and they had one son, William Francis Carruthers of Dormont, who was also possessor of Holmends and other lands anciently belonging to his family. He married Madeline, second daughter of Frederick Turner, Esq, and their son Major F J Carruthers, is now (1905) owner of the property.

The Denbie Family

William Carruthers, second son of James, laird of Holmends, and Miss Lockhart of Lee, seems to have got Denbie from his eldest brother in 1680. He married Miss Irving, heiress of Braes, and was succeeded by his son John, who had five successors in the direct line, all called John. The last of these, the late Col John Carruthers, had three daughters, and one of them married the late Mr Richard Hetherington, and their eldest son, Dr John Hetherington Carruthers R N, succeeded to the estate. It has been sold to Mr Murray of Murraythwaite.

The Braes Family

William, the second son of William Carruthers, first of Denbie, and Miss Irving of Braes, succeeded his mother in that estate. He was succeeded by his son, Captain F Carruthers, whose son Francis sold the property to the late William Curl Esquire. A branch of the family was settled at Wormonbie or Warmanbie, but it became extinct some years ago.